bloom
in
your
darkest
hour

ROSES
BY
MOONLIGHT

nicola mar

ROSES BY MOONLIGHT

Copyright © 2018 by Nicola Mar

ISBN: 978-0-9965240-3-2

FoxDay Press
Printed in the United States of America

First Edition

when in doubt...
love

never stop searching

the moon can heal
your soul

ROSES
BY
MOONLIGHT

there is something about the stillness

and darkness of night that brings out

another creature in our beings...

a voice that cannot be heard

during the sunlight

it is the voice of jealousy

and reason

the voice of happiness

and sorrow

it is the combination of all that is

and all that will be

it is an all-knowing voice

that echoes our beliefs in

the back of our minds

wanting to reveal the truth

of time -

you must choose what to allow the

voice to tell you

if you wish to sleep with

nightmares

or dreams.

the river

it flows upstream

like my dreams on a warm

day

happy to keep

my head in the clouds

holding the rain hostage

unable to ruin

this perfect parade.

where do we go from here

damaged

is what i say

there's no forgetting

what you've done

there's no forgiving

what you've become

damaged

is what i say

but not broken.

pictures will always reflect a perfect

life

no one photographs tears, fights,

tragedies,

panic, and utter devastation

so remember that

the next time you wish

to be another based on the perfectly

curated smiles that hide behind the

pain.

heavy limbs

glued to the floor

panic attacks my soul

as my feet drag

i call to you to save me

but i can't travel back in time

i'm left on this earth

without a dime

the nights are hard

when i can't make you reappear

nothing helps ease this fear

the only stillness that can

creep into my heart

is the moonlight -

a magical creature

that gives a new start.

tell me dear

where you wish to go

for i shall follow

in spirit

watching you smile

at the small things in life

that make you happy

watching you travel where

i wanted to go

i'm not mad you see

i knew my days were limited

i'm just glad I can watch you

be happy.

here they say

this is where

you should be

here

but they don't understand that

i've woken up so many times

"here"

and nothing has changed.

if all wishes are rainbows

whatever you desire

awaits you in the future

at the end of a colorful

journey.

who wants a silenced body

that can't tell the truth;

i'll take the mind that can

speak freely any day.

all i've done is try to love

try to be happy

try to live

try to stay alive

all i've done is try to survive

don't blame me if i've made

some mistakes.

wherever you are

slow down and take in

the night's air

whether crisp and cool

or humid and warm

the night's presence

can remind you that

you don't need much

to enjoy the darkness

in the absence of light

you can feel the earth

wrap around your shoulders

and tell you all will be

okay.

you
me

me
you

him
her

her
him

they
them

them
they

we

that's all there should be.

i am all the trees

the forest my home

i am the pollen

and the broken leaves

i am the canopy

i am the breeze

i am every single one

of the loving bees

so go into the night

walk with ease

for i watch all

i am here to please.

sometimes i dream of escaping my

mind

and inhabiting yours

if only for a few hours

to comfort your racing thoughts

to plant the seeds

that bring life to your secret needs

the ones that allow you

to survive.

where can i go

to stop the flow,

that electricity

that never shuts off

i hate the noises

the bright lights

there's nothing natural about

a device that claims to have

a mind better than my own.

don't be scared darling

there's another world full of

love

stronger than our own

our goodbyes are only

for a second

until we see each other again

on the brighter side.

Opening your heart

may mean breaking it

for a short while

but that's the sacrifice we all

make when we dare

to dream of love.

lightning is a friend

through the windows i watch

wishing my arms could grow

out into the rainy fields

so i can grasp onto it

i need the jolt

to open my heart

this world is so clueless

as to what nature can provide

an empty soul.

how *do you know*

what's right for me, she asked,

and i told her the truth –

because you my friend

have only lived under the shadow

of others,

whereas i have already met

all your enemies.

SO many countries, so many years

so many moments, so many tears

so many smiles, with your touch

so many times, without much

so many sunsets, so many nights

so many laughs, so many fights

so many wonders, with you around

so many times, without your sound

so many stars, so many seas

so many wishes, so many trees

so many paths, so many choices

so many times, without our voices

so many storms, so many flowers

so many passions, so many powers

so many times, it was all wrong

but never a time, i doubted

we'd stay strong.

it's time

time to learn

time to grow

it's time

time to read

time to know

it's time

time to set sail

time to row

it's time

time to reap

the benefits

you did sow.

i watch him

i want him

i watch me

i love me

i watch us

i envy us

i repeat every day

more than

i'm wiling

to say

how lucky am i

that you came

my way.

how many times

have you listened

to the voice in your

head that makes you

do the dumbest things?

why do you keep asking

her to talk when her

opinion means nothing?

learn to quiet her

since she says the meanest

things.

get comfortable

it's a long way

to the end,

if you don't take

any shortcuts.

you will either

stay broke

and unhappy

or get rich and

unhappy

why do you think

money will solve

your broken mind?

i learned the hard way how

to cope with life and its messes -

there's really nothing a good glass of

wine

some quiet jazz

a loud laugh

a bright moon

and a naked body can't fix

if only we were all born

knowing this.

i blink and you're gone

i close my eyes and you're there

i open my eyes and you're gone

i dream and you're there

i forget you today

i think about you all day

from december to may

your name's all i can

say.

it's over –

you've stolen my mind

you've made it your home,

uninvited

it's not fair

you've taken what

belongs to

me

and i'm helpless

in getting it back.

sometimes the end

is exactly where

you need to begin.

one hundred million years

is the perfect amount of time

to spend under the warm

blankets with you

on a snowy day

there's nothing smoother

than the cracks

on your body

there's nothing else worth doing

in this life we've made our own.

you're not a piece in time,

you are time -

the beginning

the middle

the eternity.

if you are not a star-gazer

you are letting the truth

slip by.

it's here!

true love

has arrived

i can finally wash my face

of the paint

and let my bare feet heal

i can finally stop pretending

i own anything but the valuables

in a velvet lined drawer

hallelujah – i'm so happy to have

nothing but you!

times are changing

in the worst way possible

people are starving

the earth is crying

animals are dying

and you are sighing

sighing

because you're

sitting in a house

that refuses the name

home.

i am

i am

i am

i am

i am

i am

i am everything

i am anything

i'm all of it

the good

the bad

the ugly

i am

whatever the hell i want to

be.

please believe that you can change

every bit of you is a different bit than it

was the day before

you can change anything

you can be anything

you can love anything

you *are*

everything.

let love

be your

north star.

walk backward

if you have to;

you're not going

forward if

you're going in the

wrong direction.

if the journey is just

a bunch of nows

then you are

always

the destination.

i love sundays

because they are

the only day when

nothing is expected of me

i can lie in bed

in peace.

you can stomp on me

until you think i'm dead,

but when you've moved on to hurt

others,

i've only begun to grow.

tick, tick, tock

do not go in

unless you knock

my body is mine

with a key and a lock

only i decide

if it wants

to talk.

we all held hands

and the universe connected

magically

like a giant rainbow

spreading its love

from the moon

to the sea

i could see nothing but a bunch

of smiles -

strangers i loved near and far.

this moment in time

will never come again

so look around you with

curious eyes

smell the grass

or the perfume

or the baby

or the very air you breathe

and hold it inside your

flesh like you never want to

be anywhere but here,

now.

i can teach you

but you must be willing to learn

i can show you

but you must be willing to see

i can tell you stories

but you must be willing to hear

i can share secrets

but you must be willing to believe.

my eyes showed me how you left this

world but i still believed they deceived

me

time told me you were gone

but i bargained it was mistaken

your belongings told me you

no longer used them

but my memories told me otherwise

my hands swore they hadn't felt you

but my mind told me you were here

how could i not believe my senses?

sometimes being alone

is the only place you want

to be

there's nothing wrong with

loving yourself more than

any other.

someone out there

waits for you to notice

that they notice you.

when he looks at me

he looks through me

to her

when he kisses me

he pretends he is kissing her

when he lays with me

he calls to her

when he leaves me

he will leave me

for her.

it's impossible not to feel

the words he spoke

when those words

broke my heart open

shocked

like a knife to an apple

cut open with nothing

to bleed.

what are words

do they matter

or are they nothing

but noises

i'd rather live with

your actions

the strong hands

that spell love

on my body

a hundred times faster

than sound travels.

maybe i was born

knowing you

and all i had to do

was remember you

to make you appear.

lay outside and feel the grass

smell the flowers

taste the dirt

say all the things you

wished you could say

to me

but were too scared

because of the labels that

are attached to them.

he says he loves her

not me

he says he needs her

not me

he says he wants her

not me

he says he knows her

not me

he says all this

because i let him

but maybe he doesn't

know

i have my own

plans.

i can be your flower

growing wildly in the field

or confined to the vase

i can be the sweet smell

or the bright colors

i can be the weed in the lawn

or the vine around the rose

i can be all these things

or none

i will be anything you let me be

as long as you let me be something.

your reactions will always

dictate your mood

choose wisely.

i've never walked down an alley so

beautiful

everything bloomed as i stepped

everything illuminated in my path

there were wild horses

next to me

and sunlight so bright

it made me squint

with happiness

there were rainbows extending

from my toes

laughs from my mouth out

through my nose

there were whites, pinks, and blues

reds, purples and yellows

this walk was everything but mellow

the dark road

was never lonely

with you by my side.

outside,

the home was just a house

the stars only fire

the moon a reflection

of what the sun had destroyed

when everything was lost

she was just a girl

under the night's sky.

there is only one secret in this life

if you can't find it

i will tell you

do not long for things

do not keep wishing on stars

do not wait for blessings

do not look for love

nothing is so great as loving

everything

you already have.

we found each other

the rest of the story

doesn't matter.

ever find that space in your mind at
night

where some insight comes to you,
crawling

through the darkness like some kind of
being?

perhaps that is what we call God

perhaps nothing is coming to us at all

perhaps we are using the quiet gap in
time

to realize we already have the answers

they have lived with us all

...all this time.

nothing hurts so great

than when you find out

he's not right for you

but somewhere inside

you already knew

i know you're listening

you know what to do.

i know you're reading this

wondering where these words

were first spoken

i don't own them

that's for sure

i'm just borrowing them

for this writing

then they will return to

us all.

what do you do

when you hate what you do

why can't you just leave

who has forced you to work on things

that are so uninteresting

who is it that said

they have power over you

because they supply money

what is money anyway

except something that burns up

into nothing

you don't burn up into nothing,

you are something

if they don't value you

maybe it's time

you leave.

here we are --

years have gone by

for a while i did

think i would die

but what a blessing

you turned out to be

you showed us all

what we needed to see.

do not focus on your past

it is a life already lived

your future is brighter

than anything holding you back.

it's little,

so small

you may never find it

but if you keep

looking

i promise

it will be worth your while

for the mind has a way

to allow your spirit

to stay.

cold fingers

that were once hot

frowns

that were once smiles

eyes

that once sparkled

bodies

that were once exciting

it all seems pointless in the end

until

until you meet someone that makes

you feel alive again

...hang on.

the silence

played the most beautiful music

in my ears tonight

drowning out all the voices in my

head

it played and played

and played

oh how beautiful it was

when you walked in the room

and chose me.

i kept you around way too long

but when you left

i realized the gift you gave me

the gift of wisdom

and i loved myself for the first time

in my life.

now i can sleep effortlessly

knowing you no longer

pull my strings.

when the pain went away

i missed it

it was a part of me you see

it kept me grounded

because being free to fly

can be scary.

poetry is for all those

who want to come home

but don't know which

direction to travel.

waking up next to you

is a greater accomplishment

than anything i have ever done

boy does it make me proud

of myself.

remember when it was so important

and so disappointing when it

didn't work out

remember how you felt

thinking life was over

just when you thought it would

get better

remember when waking up day after

day felt like a prison sentence

remember how

... somehow

the years passed

and what seemed so devastating

was worth laughing at

remember those feelings

when your heart bleeds again.

maybe it wasn't meant to be

but maybe

we should just wait and see.

no matter how many

words i write

new ones keep being

born

no matter how many

thoughts i erase

new ones keep

calling.

a wave in the ocean

a raindrop from the clouds

a splash in the pond

somehow all the water ripples in this

world seem to have come from my

eyes.

how many ways can i scramble

different words

to tell you

he's not worth it

how many sentences can i form

to make you realize you are

wasting your time

how many poems can i write

to show you how powerful

you really are

how many years will it take

until you see the truth

in all these pages?

come on darling

there's a sky

full of stars

just waiting for us

to claim them.

certain nights call for

certain adventures.

if your world could speak

it would tell you that

you're doing an okay job

not just okay,

you are doing a good job

you're out there inserting

your beliefs into humanity

just promise me

you won't hurt

people

along the way.

stop! i yelled after he had turned

around

you've gone too far and i miss you

already.

i bought everything

because i could afford it

i spent my life collecting things

i saw others have

now you must be happy, my mind

whispered

but i went home

and all i wanted

was a kiss from you

the things sat in the closet

aging

year after year

wishing they could fall in love

like i had.

"**i** have no regrets"

doesn't it feel so wonderful

to say

doesn't it make all the

feelings melt away

try it with me,

say it today.

as i write

i remember the night

we had our worst fight

i had sight

but no light

bitter with envy

consumed with spite

i should have held tight

let go of my might

but instead

i just had to be right.

the photo reveals her scars,

but not her suffering.

light as a feather

let me go

and i shall float away with the wind

pushing me through the clouds

watching over all below me

letting them experience what

i already know.

do not focus on your past

it is a life already lived

your future is brighter

than anything holding you

back.

what makes a home your own?

surely it can't be the walls you paid for,

for those walls can come down at any

moment

it is the love we share within that space

for if the walls disappeared,

our love would only expand.

we all suffer greatly

but those who learn

to express it

flourish,

deeply in love with the

art that stems from

their own pain.

i swore i'd never find the love

i deserved

so i kept searching in

places and in people i knew didn't

matter

it was a reflex that had been

conditioned

out of fear

because no one in this world

ever told me to be free.

only the poet

knows what the words

are feeling

only the reader

knows how to comfort

them.

the woman asked me what i learned

from what you did to me

i said nothing

you brought nothing to my life

and she smiled

"do you know there's a 'thing' in

nothing?"

you can

ALWAYS

take back

your power

at any

moment.

birds

they keep singing

no matter who has tried to

silence them.

when i had almost given up

i met someone who showed me

that my value

could not be measured

i was, am, and always will be

the most important part of

my world.

have you ever felt a better feeling

than floating slowly

under a wave warmed by the blinding

sun?

if you close your eyes and recreate the

feeling in your mind

i promise you

i'll be there to help you to the surface.

if your tears grew gardens

in your mind

maybe they were worth

shedding.

give everything you have to give

and watch how much will float back

to you

love in every way you can

and feel how much will

cling to you

believe in yourself

and see how much

you will accomplish.

do not make them own you

leave if you have to

fight if you need to

do everything to protect your

passion

do not give up on what you

know you can contribute

i believe in your gifts

and i think they are the most

wonderful part of you.

the sad songs produce tears of joy

pain is the best thing that ever

happened to me

it will be the best thing that has ever

happened to you

just give it time.

if you get lost in this world

just let yourself wander

until you find your new

home.

if love is power

i will always be

your queen.

when i lost you

i closed my eyes and

you appeared

we traveled down the dirt road

together

it was fall and leaves littered the ground

and crunched under our feet

a mess of earth and spirit and memories

it was what you said to me that day

that made my happiness appear once

again

perhaps even stronger than before you

left

you assured me

i would never again feel the pain i felt

the day you went away

that pain had come

had gone

had actualized itself

that pain opened my mind to how real

the pain was

and facing it

made me become friends with it

because i had created it.

all i ever need to do now is

believe that you can appear

at any moment

and you are there.

you don't always have to search for

your feelings

sometimes you just need to feel them.

there was never a part of you i missed

because i had traced every part of your

body with my hands for years

i could feel any part of your body in my

mind whenever i wanted.

sometimes

forever just isn't enough

sometimes

i want more.

there is no definition of impossible

it's a made-up word to scare you

control you

dominate you

keep you from being happy

let go of the meaning...

late at night

is when my mind

decides it will wander to you

there we meet

in the air

able to share what we feel

together in spirit

is where we belong

i shall meet you in flesh

again someday

until then

let's keep our late night

appointments.

and then i finally

saw it...

my beauty

...and i was so happy

it was mine to keep.

i will always speak the truth

even it means being ridiculed

for that is always better than being

muzzled.

the piano plays by itself

making the walls

fall in love with the

space in between.

that clean air filled with invisible

words lingering in sweet

memories

there's no need for you

to be here

when i can remember

everything about you

and our time

so vividly.

around you

all the shooting stars

in the sky

are inside me.

always lend your voice to others

who struggle

one day

they will be strong enough

to lend their voices to you

when you are

silenced.

trust that things happen

for a reason

you may not be able to see through

the fog right now

but trust

that everything will reveal itself

in time

be patient.

i can't imagine

that anyone

could love you

more than i do

in this moment

in time.

afterall,

we

lived

to

tell

the

story

and laugh about it.

we were born

loving life

what happened along

the way

does not need to define

the rest of

our lives.

i just don't understand

how we could be

so perfectly perfect

for each other.

say what you will

your words will

just wash away

like the hurt you

thought would stick.

if you need to,

just blame me,

you are hurting,

i'll help you float.

i still smile

when i don't

get my way

because i know that

sometimes

giving and taking

means a little more

giving

than

taking.

you don't have to look

a certain way

to fit in

try to fit your personality to

your look

and become an original.

through the support of others

we cause wars

but smile with another

and slowly peace

will spread

one person at a time

knowing another in

all honesty -

raw and loving.

don't settle for so little

when the world waits

for you to take

so much.

you have talents

that others are jealous of

don't waste them

run away into the night

and seize what belongs

to you.

sleepless nights

taught me to love

my soul.

some nights we make love

some nights we fight

but we always have each other

in the end.

give what you can

when you can

ask nothing in return

that's all there is

to what we know as living.

sometimes

it feels like vines wrap

around your legs

preventing you from moving

sometimes

it feels like balloons

are tied to your shoulders

allowing you to travel to the clouds

sometimes you can't get out of bed

and sometimes you can't wait to.

who are you?

life will bring the right people

to you

at the right time.

trust this.

the pain will stick around

long after you leave

but i won't let it destroy me

like you did.

many do not see the sun rise in the

morning

but just knowing it's there

willing to wake up every morning for

you

should tell you

that you, too, can get through this

the universe is on your side.

this year, dream bigger

say what you feel

do what you've always longed to do

rest longer than normal

eat more of what makes you happy

call bullshit when you see it

and don't let people get you down

you are special

you have something important

to contribute

you have a voice

a special soul

it's time to use it

surround yourself with love

and give every fiber of your being

to others who need it.

every artist knows

the hands always create

the truth even when

the mind is too scared

to think.

it was may

when she took you away

end of spring

when you had that fling

i'll never forgive you

for making me blue

for using me

and her too

but now i have a new friend.

ever bury your toes in the sand

and wish the sun could shine on

your face for eternity?

ever wish the bright moon

could wash away your pain?

ever wish all the things

you've acquired in life

were not things at all?

ever wish you could take

back time

so you could stand tall?

time is not waiting for you

to make up your mind

time is laughing at you

right now

because you think

there's a perfect

opportunity

in the future -

but

there is only

now.

the music that played

made me cry

for the first time in years

i understood how being alone

could make me so happy.

we all have choices to make

why not choose love

instead of hate

why not wander

instead of rush

why not pack your bags

and travel to the town

with the yellow weeds

and broken-down houses

full of laughter

why not quit your job

and follow your passion

why not lead others

to stop pretending all is well

when it's broken

why not say yes

instead of no?

it wasn't like me

not to flee when

you disrespected

me

but your love was something

i could not break

for your sake

you were lost

and i knew i could

save you.

and with your words

i slept deeply

knowing they were mine

forever

for nothing could take back

that moment when

the gift from your voice

brought another world

to my dreams.

please don't ever think

you can't change -

go into the sea

fly to the moon

climb the mountain

there's no such thing

as doom

for all will learn

the truth

soon.

i'm thinking of you

as i write these words

it's late at night

and i can only hear

your voice in my head

telling me i'd be okay

i'd flourish without you

i still see you every day

and all i do is pretend i'm okay

because it's what you

told me to say.

i can try to protect you

but you will get hurt

you will hurt so badly

you'll claw at your body

trying to break free

of the skin that

surrounds you

hoping that if you

managed to slip away

there'd be something

wonderful waiting for you

on the other side

but if you hang on

and deal with all those pieces

of you

i know you'll come out of the

storm more powerful

than when you went in.

revenge

is what i crave

for everything you

put me through

i stay awake at night

listing the ways you

deceived me

and all i want to do is scream

at the top of my lungs

until i hate myself for being so

stupid

until i hate myself more

than i hate you

but at the end of a long darkness

the sun rises

jolting my eyes awake when i

hadn't realized i dozed

off

the pain has subsided,

all i want is your touch again.

your hand in mind

your kiss on my forehead

i need you again

and i can't think of anything

better than feeling your

feet under the sheets.

she may look

pretty on the outside

but her heart is ice,

not even close to the sun

that resides

in my chest.

i will love you

until the waves die

and even then

without movement

we'll be together as one.

happiest when there's

nothing to worry about

except how we will spend

the weekends with

each other.

rock bottom

is not hard at all -

an easy place

for a new beginning

sky high

is not blue at all -

an easy place

to see the end

the mundane

is not routine at all -

an easy place

for us to appreciate each other.

you are the young memories

when life was as carefree as

the crickets that sung and the

warm sea we danced in

you are the days that can never

be replaced --

by money or travel, by age

or wisdom

you are the memory of a

life when adventure was always

on the horizon and simple was

foolishly taken for granted

you are the space in my mind

that reminds me to look up at

the stars, knowing that you

might still be looking

up too.

you can start right now

all you have to do is

decide.

all i need is

a coffee

a dog

an afternoon filled

with sunlight

in a bed with a silky

comforter

that i can hide under

with you.

when all the world is crying

be the smile that breaks

the tears

be the light

that makes the darkness

aware of its beauty

be the leaf that dances despite

its demise

be the creature

that no one can define

because of its difference.

a body of

scars

shines

like the night's

stars.

i will never get used to the sunset

that sparkles over the sea

i will never get used to the rainbow that

touches eternity.

all that really

matters

is that your

loved ones

are safe

happy

and healthy

all that other

stuff

is just an illusion

of

importance.

do not go down

without fighting

for what you believe

in

do not run out

without saying what

you're feeling

do not lay down

when you're

still breathing.

in the middle of the woods

sat a ladybug on a tree

i could have sworn it

smiled at me

and just as i was

about to approach

it spread its wings

to jump on my brooch

so i walked around

with a bug on my shirt

and for a moment in time

i forgot all the hurt.

you can always choose

to leave words in the past

and replace their meanings

with new ones.

try to play me

like an instrument

or a dummy

or both

try to play me

if you're willing to

take the risk.

i sit in the dark room

with walls closing in

on my body

i sit in the dark room

that's my mind.

i'm running through a field

the music gets louder and louder

as i approach the end

i can smell the newly cut grass

and hear the songs of the birds

who encourage me to come near

finally i can see you in the distance

you twirl and call to me

waving your hands in the air

i can almost smell your hair

and feel your soft skin

oh it's like the petals after

a light rain

i'm coming to you

i am almost home.

it was always worth it

no matter what happened

in the end

you are my greatest mistake

and my most glorious

memory.

don't let them tell you

that you're not pretty

enough

pretty grows inside you

every morning

with every deep breath

you become more

beautiful than you were

the moment before.

just find your passion

and live it.

i know this reads like

a sad love song

but sometimes those

songs can inspire you

because you know

there's someone else

who feels exactly the way

you do right now

you are never alone

and you never will be.

it is with great pride

that i say i left you

it is with great strength

that i say i miss you

it is with great reason

that i say i don't need you

it is with great accomplishment

that i say i forgive you.

i can fly while i'm falling

i can breathe while i'm drowning

i can float while i'm sinking

i can die while i'm living.

meeting you gave me the
courage

to let go of all my fears.

that's it -

i've found the word for you

you

are

magic.

the window let the light in

but kept my fears from escaping

i was too scared to open the latch

in fear i might have to face the

unknown

the routine was too familiar

to give up.

sometimes

you meet magical people

who inspire you

to do everything you

never thought possible.

the snow

fell slowly

silencing

the new york city

streets

for the first time in years

i felt its energy.

so much

love

so little

time.

you don't have to wait

for a new day to start

anew

you can do that

in every

moment.

there is nothing that feels better than

sitting in a warm bubble bath

petting a sleepy puppy

drinking a warm cup of tea

or basking in the sunlight

under the watchful eyes

of the sea waves

you see

the best and most

satisfying things in life

will always be things that

evoke a deep nostalgia

for a pleasant feeling

in the soul.

the bird

does not romance

the flower that is sour -

it simply goes to the

one that is

sweet.

busy breathing.

come back later.

why do we

choose poison

when there's

so much elixir

in our sight?

sewing my mouth

shut will not

prevent my hands

from telling the

truth.

his words have become

a quiet hum

that i pretend is the

wind whistling on a

sunny day

his smile has become

a stitched emotion

that i pretend is the result

of happiness.

opening your heart

does not have to involve

any sort of suffering.

nothing is better than

your voice

whispering in my ear

from

thousands of miles away

i can sleep soundly tonight.

long after it was over

we lay together

hugging each other

because these bodies

were once one

sharing everything inside

them

we refused to forget the love

even long after it was over.

love is never gone

it just takes time

to realize that

even through the

mourning of being

apart -- love

is still there

lingering.

i could tell when you left

you didn't want to

i knew i could

convince you to stay

but

i knew it was best

not to.

writing is magic

it makes me remember it all,

it also makes it disappear.

my mind does not work

like a book

flipping pages

i remember everything

that happened

all at once

telling me you love me

won't make me forget

the pain you caused.

i let my hair be free

rolling past my shoulders

tickling my back

i let my skin be bare

my green eyes

the only color on it

i let my body be naked

as i walked into the ocean

the sun as my only witness.

it's a shame

we change so many things

about our differences,

the small but courageous lips

the wrinkles that hold memories

the attitudes that define us,

because there's nothing

on our bodies

or in our minds

that will ever match our souls.

if you'll teach me

i'll take all your lessons

on how to love you.

why she lived

is so much more

important

than why she died.

you don't get to put

me in your shadows,

to hold me back from

my passions

because you think you

are more important.

if only you knew

controlling another

will lead to your own

demise.

10 years passed

and i could still smell

you on my clothes

sometimes it's a blessing

sometimes it's a curse.

you went away so quickly

i couldn't process what

happened

but i did learn

one thing the hard way --

loneliness is real but necessary

if you want to live.

it wasn't what you said

it was how you delivered it.

i'd fallen

in love

so many times

i didn't know

how

to fly.

words are potions,

if ingested

they will

heal

or they will

kill.

love does not have a timeline

love was there before you

discovered it

love will last

even after you've left it.

looking back,

there was so much i

didn't understand about you

and so much i wish i had

perhaps we could have years back

if i had only accepted that

you weren't in love with me

the way i was with

you.

it's magical

in a world of billions

when you find your soul

mate

your eyes meet and in an

instant you know that

you have loved this

person for many

lifetimes before

you know that all of life

has finally made sense,

has led you to this moment,

to be with this person

forever

your heart skips a beat,

thinking for a second that

you had come across the one

in luck --

not realizing that the whole world

conspired to take you here at this

very moment.

don't be particular

when it comes to love

lose all the labels

and start feeling love

from a mystical level.

i follow you

like the sun across the earth

i follow you

hoping you'll dictate

my worth

i follow you

through rain and shine

i follow you

hoping you'll be mine

i follow you

through the day

until i realize

there's nothing

left to pray

for i've followed you

for my whole life

and what's followed me

was only your strife.

i would spear the sun

to bring you

the light

i would capture

the stars spread

through the night

i would reach into

the fire that would

blind my sight

i would do anything

to kill your fright

just trust me,

hold tight.

there's a place for you

in this world

if only you would trust

what makes you smile.

most of the time

we hang on

because it feels

safe

when in reality

letting go would

be so much

less toxic.

if all you ever said

was thank you,

you will have lived

a life that's

worthwhile.

rage comes in the middle

of the night

sleep deprived i imagine

all the scenarios

that don't fit with what

i've planned for us

my head hits the pillow over

and over, killing any chance

of entering the dream world

and just when i'm about

to explode

the air leaves my lungs

my eyes collapse

and the sun shines,

washing away

the thoughts that

roam my wild

mind.

sometimes we wear heels

sometimes we need to heal.

words -

they walk the wild terrain

fighting with my

thoughts -

my mind a battlefield

for the letters who only

wish to rearrange

to form

LOVE.

he didn't just say it

he felt it

but sometimes

those feelings fade,

too.

would you wish

for things

or for

wings?

where does it all go

the pain that stabs me

but subsides

with time

where does it all go

does it force its way out

of the universe

only to die

or has it traveled to

another?

he appeared

and my skin

felt at home

in his presence.

you will find out

that mean people

often wear fake

smiles.

when i finally realized

i could fly

there was no need to

stay on earth

for there was far more

beauty above

the clouds.

they can hurt you

but they can never

take away the love

you possess.

it doesn't matter when

you gave it away

you can always get your

power back

the minute you decide

to reclaim it.

she was nothing that needs fixing

she was everything that was

already perfect

except for her mind.

i let

him hurt me over and over

again

like the ocean that just can't

get enough of the shore

always reaching out for more

i'm not proud of it

but i've moved on.

the silence

can be a beautiful

space

if you're willing

to hear the words

it whispers.

never put yourself last

always see yourself

winning.

she didn't know that fire

caused scars

she only knew

she was willing to put

up with the pain.

i see so much when i close my eyes

that sometimes i fear i

don't want to wake

i want to continue to dance with you

the way things used to be

i don't want to wake to cold sheets,

lost love,

and a whole lot

of heartache.

you

can

be

bold

if

you

decide

to

try.

there were amazing times

where you felt like you could fly

and nobody could take away your

wings no matter how many times

they tried to break you

and there were terrible times

where curling up and throwing up

and giving up were the only

options in front of you

but then there were ordinary times

-- the routines, the smiles, the warm

night's air,

the birds that sang outside your

window,

and the sun that rose for you

every morning

and all of those things made up your

year, but it is the ones you choose to

remember that will guide you through

the next

so remember the ordinary as

extraordinary because they are

the ones you will continue

to see the most --

and they are the ones that will

keep you calm during the storm

and grateful during all the

magic.

ABOUT THE AUTHOR

Nicola Mar grew up on the Caribbean island of St. Maarten, where she wrote her first short story at age seven. At eighteen, Nicola moved to the U.S. to continue her education, graduating from Rollins College with a bachelor's degree in anthropology and a specialty in creative writing. Roses by Moonlight is Nicola's third poetry collection. Nicola currently lives in New York City with her two dogs. Visit her website at **www.nicolamar.com**

OTHER BOOKS BY NICOLA

A Red Tale

Santa;

Haiku Hive

Figments

FOLLOW NICOLA ONLINE

www.instagram.com/nicolamar

www.facebook.com/nicolamar

www.twitter.com/nicolamar